# CHANGING WORLD
# PAKISTAN

# CHANGING WORLD

# PAKISTAN

**David Abbott**

ARCTURUS

This edition first published in 2010 by Arcturus Publishing
Distributed by Black Rabbit Books
P.O. Box 3263
Mankato
Minnesota MN 56002

Printed in China

Library of Congress Cataloging-in-Publication Data

Abbott, David, 1960-
  Pakistan / David Abbott.
     p. cm. -- (Changing world)
  Includes index.
  ISBN 978-1-84837-644-1 (library bound)
  1. Pakistan--Juvenile literature. I. Title.

  DS376.9.A23 2011
  954.91--dc22

                          2009051187

Series concept: Alex Woolf
Editor: Jacqueline McCann
Designer: Ian Winton
Maps and charts: Stefan Chabluk
Picture researcher: Jacqueline McCann

Picture credits:
Bridgeman: 11 (Johnson Album I/British Library/British Library Board).
Corbis: cover left (Michele Falzone/JAI), 3 (Christophe Boisvieux), 9 (Annie Griffiths Belt),
10 (Diego Lezama Orezzoli), 12 (Jane Sweeney/JAI), 13 & 14 (Bettmann),
16 (Kapoor Baldev), 17 top (Jonathan Blair), 17 bottom (STR/PAKISTAN/Reuters),
19 (Rajat Dar), 22 (T. Mughal/epa), 25 (Rehan Khan/epa), 28 & 34 (Nadim Khawer/epa),
37 Christine Osborne, 39 (Pakistan Military Dept.), 41 (Robert Harding).
Getty: cover right (Arif Ali/AFP), 8 (Eric Feferberg), 15 (Popperfoto), 18, 20, 23 & 42 (Arif Ali/Stringer),
21 (AFP/Stringer), 24 (ARKO DATTA/AFP), 27 (Aamir Qureshi/AFP), 30 (Keren Su), 31, 32 & 35
(Aamir Qureshi/Stringer), 33 (Chris Hondros), 36 (Paula Bronstein), 38 (Liu Jin/AFP), 40 (Spencer Platt).
Flickr: 26 (Remy Steinegger/World Economic Forum), 43 (Michael Gross).
Wikipedia: 29.

Cover captions:
Left: Badshadi Mosque, Lahore, Pakistan.
Right: Pakistani models showing the summer collection of designers from the Pakistan Fashion Designers Council.

ISBN: 978-1-84837-644-1
SL001314US
Supplier 03, Date 0210

# Contents

# CHAPTER 1

# Introduction

The Islamic Republic of Pakistan is wedged between central Asia and the Indian subcontinent. It is flanked by Afghanistan and Iran on the west and China and India on the east. This large country occupies what has always been strategically important land, controlling access through the mountains between central Asia and the Indian subcontinent. For hundreds of years, the history of this region has been shaped by waves of foreign invaders. Ever since the modern state of Pakistan was founded in 1947, it has had to make alliances with its neighbors and other powerful nations.

This history has had a big impact on Pakistan. It has made it a country with many diverse ethnic groups, with their own religious beliefs, languages, and ways of life. All these factors and recent economic growth make Pakistan a land of sharp contrasts and social tensions.

## Landscape

The north and west of Pakistan are dominated by the Karakoram and Hindu Kush mountain ranges. One of the most famous peaks is K2, the world's second-highest mountain at 28,244 feet (8,611 metres, m). More mountain ranges lie to the southwest in Balochistan. In the central area of the country, the mountain ranges end and the fertile Indus plain is the key feature of the landscape. Farther to the east lie three areas of desert: the Thar Desert in Sindh and the Thal and Cholistan deserts in Punjab. The Indus River flows into the Arabian Sea south of Karachi, forming a swampy delta and floodplain.

## Climate

Pakistan's climate is generally dry and arid, but there are big differences between the north and south of the country. More than 75 percent of Pakistan has less than 9.8 inches (25 centimeters, cm) of rainfall per year, which means irrigation is needed for agriculture. Summer

**COMPARING COUNTRIES: HOW BIG IS PAKISTAN?**

Pakistan is roughly four times larger than the United Kingdom (UK) and only 8 percent the size of the US. It has the world's sixth-largest population and the second- biggest Muslim population.

| Country | Land area in square miles | Population in millions |
|---------|---------------------------|------------------------|
| US | 3,832,386 | 307 |
| India | 1,282,160 | 1,148 |
| Pakistan | 313,537 | 166 |
| France | 213,330 | 65 |
| Germany | 139,230 | 82 |
| UK | 95,480 | 60 |

Note: 1 square mile = 2.60 square kilometers

Source: CIA *World Factbook*

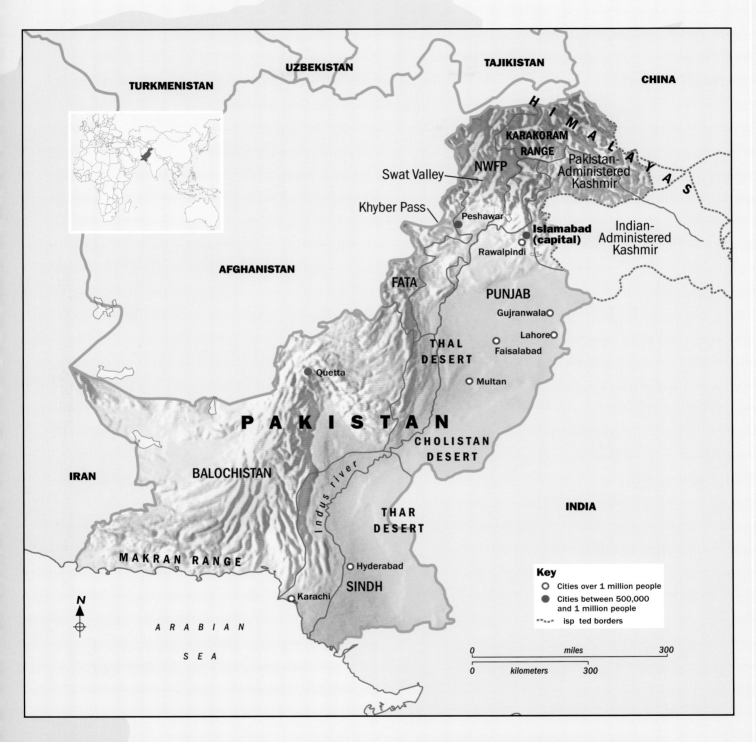

**Key**
- ○ Cities over 1 million people
- ● Cities between 500,000 and 1 million people
- --- isp ted borders

0         miles        300

0        kilometers       300

temperatures in the southern plains are usually 95 to 104 degrees Fahrenheit (°F) (35 to 40 degrees Celcius, °C) but can reach 122 °F (50°C). Between June and October, much of the country undergoes the rainy monsoon season. In winter, temperatures in the south are around 84°F (29°C).

**Pakistan is made up of four main provinces: Balochistan in the south, Sindh to the southeast, Punjab to the east, and the North-West Frontier Province (NWFP) to the north.**

In the mountains, it is very cold and the temperature can drop to 20°F (-29 °C).

## A variety of cultures

Pakistan is divided into four main provinces (see map page 7) and three smaller territories: the Federally Administered Tribal Areas (FATA), the Northern Areas, and the Islamabad Capital Territory. These provinces and territories are home to a great diversity of ethnic groups. Predominant are the Punjabis, but there are other important ethnic groups such as the Pashtuns, Sindhis, Muhajirs, and Balochis. All of these ethnic groups can be subdivided, and there are many smaller groups.

## Punjabis

The Punjabis make up the largest ethnic group, accounting for 60 percent of the population of Pakistan. The Punjab is situated in eastern

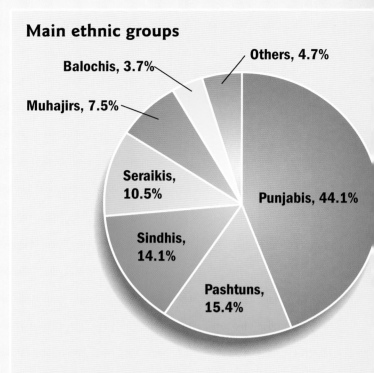

**Main ethnic groups**

- Others, 4.7%
- Balochis, 3.7%
- Muhajirs, 7.5%
- Seraikis, 10.5%
- Punjabis, 44.1%
- Sindhis, 14.1%
- Pashtuns, 15.4%

Source: Government of Pakistan, Federal Bureau of Statistics

Pakistan, but the region also extends across the border into northwest India. Traditionally, the Punjabis have been farmers and solidiers, dominating the officer class of Pakistan's army.

## The Pashtuns

The Pashtuns (or Pathans) live in northeast Pakistan and are thought to originate from eastern Iran. Pashtuns are the second-largest ethnic group in Pakistan, although many also live in Afghanistan. Many Pashtuns serve in the armed forces.

## Sindhis, Muhajir and Baloch

Sindhis come from southern Pakistan, and many, such as the Bhutto family, have prominent roles in political life. Another important group is the Muhajir, an Urdu-

**This elderly Pashtun man comes from the mountains of northern Pakistan and is dressed for the cold winter. Pashtun men often dye their beards orange using henna.**

speaking group that migrated to Pakistan when it became an independent state in 1947. This group has often dominated official positions within the state administration. The Baloch live in the southwest, near Iran. Balochistan is the largest province in Pakistan, although many people in the region have sought independence from Pakistan for some time.

## Languages

The fact that there are about six main languages and a total of approximately 80 languages spoken in Pakistan gives some idea of the diversity of cultures within the country. Most Pakistanis speak or understand the official language, Urdu, as well as one other language. English is used as the official administrative language, further complicating matters. Language has often been a matter of considerable political importance in Pakistan. In 1962, Sindhis protested when Urdu was made a compulsory subject in elementary schools. In 1972, Prime Minister Zulfikar Bhutto made the study of Sindhi compulsory, provoking protests by Urdu-speaking Mujahirs.

In 1947, many Bengalis in East Pakistan wanted Bengali to be the joint national language alongside Urdu. Protests and riots followed when Urdu was declared the sole national language. Despite all these differences, the languages of Pakistan have many shared elements. Most of the languages are written using the Arabic alphabet and have common linguistic roots.

**These women are from the Sindh province of southern Pakistan. Like most Pakistani women, they wear the national dress of *shalwar kameez*, pajama-like pants and a long shirt, with a head scarf, called a dupatta.**

# CHAPTER 2

# History

Pakistan, standing at the gateway to central Asia, has been invaded and settled by many different armies throughout its history. At one time or another, it has been invaded by Persians, Aryans, Greeks, Scythians, Arabs, Huns, and also the British.

## Ancient civilizations

The first settlements in Pakistan date to about 6500 BCE, when Pakistan was populated by Neolithic farming communities. By 3000 BCE, the Indus Valley was populated by many farming communities. The remains of two cities from around this time have been found at Mohenjo-Daro in Sindh and Harappa in the Punjab. Both cities contained sophisticated brick buildings, an administrative center, an efficient sewage system, and neatly ordered residential areas. Sometime between 1900 and 1800 BCE, what is known as the Indus Valley

### KEY DATES IN PAKISTAN'S EARLY HISTORY

6500–5000 BCE Agriculture established in the Indus Valley
2600–1800 BCE Indus Valley Civilization
514 BCE Persians invade
326 BCE Alexander the Great invades
c. 711 Arabs introduce Islam
1526 The Mughal dynasty begins

**The site of Mohenjo-Daro, or Mound of the Dead, was discovered in Pakistan in the 1920s. This ancient city of the Indus Valley Civilization flourished between 2600 and 1900 BCE.**

This image depicts the first Mughal emperor, Babur, at the head of his army. Babur engaged in many battles to dominate central Asia and the Indian subcontinent.

Civilization seems to have declined, though the causes are not clear. It is thought that the Indus river changed course and several earthquakes occurred. This could explain why the civilization died out.

## Early invaders

After the decline of the Indus Valley Civilization, Pakistan came under the influence of semi-nomadic Aryan tribes migrating from central Asia. In the fifth century BCE, Pakistan was part of the Persian Empire, and by the fourth century BCE, it was conquered by Alexander the Great.

For the next few centuries, Pakistan was subject to more invasions and a succession of dynasties and empires: Scythians, Kushans, Sassanians, and Huns. By the sixth century CE, Pakistan already had a rich and complex history, but the arrival of the Islamic faith in the seventh century CE was to have an important and long-lasting influence.

## The coming of Islam

The Muslim faith was first brought to Pakistan by Arab invaders led by Muhammad bin Qasim in about 711. Before that, Hinduism and Buddhism were important religions, but Islam spread quickly through the region once it was introduced. By the fifteenth century, Islam was well established as a major religion in the country.

## The Mughal Empire

Of all the dynasties and empires in Pakistan's early history, the Mughal Empire is perhaps best known. The first of the Mughal (the word comes from *Mongol*) emperors, Babur, descended from the Mongol leader Ghengis Khan. He swept through the Khyber Pass with his army in 1526 and defeated the last of the Delhi sultans at the Battle of Panipat. At the height of their power in 1700, the Mughal dynasty controlled most of the Indian subcontinent. The six Mughal emperors introduced the game of polo, built fine forts and palaces, and also created an administrative system that helped create the building blocks of a modern state: a tax system, roads, and a well-organized army.

## European dominance

By the sixteenth century, several European powers were competing for trade and territory in Pakistan and India. The French, Dutch, Portuguese, and British all jostled for dominance in the region. It was the British, though, who emerged as the dominant power around the middle of the eighteenth century.

## British rule

British involvement in India and Pakistan began in 1615, when a company called the East India Company started exporting cotton and tea to Britain. The East India Company became very successful and even built fortresses throughout the country in order to protect its trading posts. The British government sent troops to the region but did not seize direct political control until after

### CASE STUDY: THE GREAT GAME

In the nineteenth century, Russia was eager to extend its territory across central Asia. Britain feared the Russians might attack India through the Khyber Pass. Both sides engaged in military and diplomatic activity in order to try to achieve dominance in the region. The Pamir mountains were a key point of tension, but an agreement in 1895 established the Wakhan Corridor as a buffer zone between Pakistan and Russia.

the Great Mutiny of 1857–58, when Indian troops attacked the British. After 1858, the British governed Pakistan and India through a viceroy (governor) appointed by the monarch.

**The Khyber Pass is a 33-mile (53-kilometer, km) passage through the Hindu Kush mountains. It connects the northern frontier of Pakistan with Afghanistan and so is a key route to the "stans"—Uzbekistan, Tajikistan, and Turkmenistan, then Kazakhstan and on to Russia.**

**Ali Jinnah (1876–1948) was the first governor-general of Pakistan and the country's founding father.**

**Mahatma Gandhi (1869–1948) led a successful campaign of non-violent resistance against British rule in India and was the foremost leader of the Indian independence movement.**

## British influence

The British are credited with helping to modernize and develop Pakistan during their rule. Under the British, railways were developed and the canals that helped to irrigate the Punjab were repaired and extended, making more land available for cultivation. However, British rule caused tensions. In the Punjab, landowners, who tended to be Hindus, did well under British rule, but many peasants, who were Muslims, felt they were unfairly treated. This deepened tensions that already existed between Hindus and Muslims.

## The Muslim League and independence

Tensions between Muslims and Hindus developed through the nineteenth century and led to the creation of a group called the Muslim League in 1906. The founders of the Muslim League believed that Muslim interests and rights were being neglected and campaigned to improve the situation. They also tried to work with activists campaigning for an independent India. For some time in the 1920s, it seemed possible that an independent India would include the territory of what is now Pakistan. However, Muslim League president Ali Jinnah lost confidence that Muslims would be treated fairly. He believed that Muslims and Hindus were two different nations and required two separate states: the "Two Nation Theory." In the period before Indian independence in 1947, Jinnah rejected calls for unity from Indian leader Mahatma Gandhi.

## Independence

Ali Jinnah rejected Gandhi's call for the creation of a united India, and on August 14, 1947, Pakistan was designated an independent state and member of the British Commonwealth. Muhammad Ali Jinnah was appointed its first governor-general and led Pakistan for the first year of its nationhood.

## Birth of a nation

The announcement of independence for Pakistan led to widespread violence between Muslims and Hindus. This led many Hindus and Sikhs to leave Pakistan for India, while many Muslims living in India traveled in the opposite direction. The Pakistan authorities estimated that 8 million Muslims moved into Pakistan and 6 million Hindus left for India. As many as a million people may have died in the violence that accompanied the first months of independence.

## A divided country

The new state of Pakistan consisted of two parts: East and West Pakistan, but these regions were separated by Indian territory. West Pakistan, the larger part of the country, was a thousand miles away from East Pakistan, which lay on the Bay of Bengal. The distance between the two parts of the country and the fact that India divided the two areas made it difficult to govern effectively. Added to this were cultural and political tensions. East Pakistanis wanted Bengali to be their official language, but Pakistan's early leaders always insisted that Urdu would remain the official national language.

## Wars with India

The partition of India and Pakistan into separate states led not just to cross-border violence between Muslims and Hindus, but disputes over border territory. One important case was that of Kashmir. In 1948, Pakistan entered the territory to defend local Muslims and supported a guerrilla war against Kashmir's maharaja (ruler). India also intervened at the request

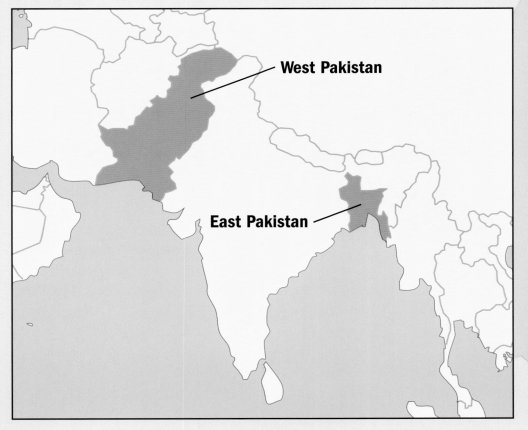

**West Pakistan**

**East Pakistan**

**This map shows East and West Pakistan, which together in 1947 formed the new state of Pakistan. Between them lay 1,000 miles (1,610 km) of Indian territory which is why they were also known as the East Wing and the West Wing.**

In 1971, India went to war with Pakistan. Here, Pakistani soldiers in East Pakistan study a map of the region, just a few miles from the border with India.

of the Kashmiri prime minister to defend the territory against Pakistan. A cease-fire was established, but the dispute was not resolved, and there was a short period of fighting again in 1965. In 1971, the disagreements between East and West Pakistan erupted into a civil war. India invaded and forced Pakistan to surrender in December 1971. The new independent state of Bangladesh, formed out of the old East Pakistan, was declared shortly afterward. The war was bitterly fought, and a conference held in 2005 estimated that around 26,000 people lost their lives in the conflict.

## COMPARING COUNTRIES: PAKISTAN AND BANGLADESH

|  | Pakistan | Bangladesh |
|---|---|---|
| Population | 176 million | 156 million |
| Area | 313,560 square mi | 56,160 square mi |
| Life expectancy | 64.5 years | 60.2 years |
| Total fertility rate | 3.6 | 2.74 |
| Per capita income | $2,600 | $1,500 |
| % population below poverty line | 24% | 45% |
| Labor force by occupation | Agriculture, 43% Industry, 20% Services, 36% | Agriculture, 63% Industry, 11% Services, 26% |

Note: 1 square mile = 2.60 square kilometers

Source: CIA *World Factbook*, 2009

# CHAPTER 3

# ☪ Social Changes

**P**akistan was founded as a Muslim state, and religion has always played an important role in the country. However, religion is now a source of controversy: some traditionalists want Islam to play a greater role in politics and public life, while others prefer religion to be a private matter.

## The role of Islam

General Zia ul-Haq (1924–88) was the first leader of Pakistan to advance policies that would win the approval of Muslim radicals. Zia promoted a policy of Islamization, introducing a council that aimed to bring all Pakistan's laws into line with Islamic principles. Traditional punishments, such as flogging and stoning, were instituted for a number of crimes. New laws and policies were introduced into the economy and education systems so that they could be run according to Islamic principles.

After General Zia's death in 1988, Islamization went into decline and some policies were overturned, but this led to tension, protest, and conflict between Islamist radicals and the government. In 2009, President Zardari's government made concessions to Islamic radicals and allowed sharia law to take priority over civil law in the far north Swat Valley region.

## Education

Education is vital in a rapidly developing country, and Pakistan has an extensive system of publicly funded and private schools that aim to supply the educated workers needed in a young country. In 2005–6 Pakistan's ministry of education calculated that the country had 163,671 state schools, teaching students at six levels from preschool to degree-level studies. In a recent

**General Zia ul-Haq staged a coup in 1977 and appointed himself president in 1978. He died in an airplane crash in 1988. He had many enemies while president, and some commentators believe the crash was a deliberate act of sabotage.**

Classroom space is full at the Aga Khan Diamond Jubilee School in the Hunza region of northern Pakistan, which is why these young boys have moved outside for their lessons.

survey (2004–5) for the ministry of education, there were high levels of enrollment for state elementary education, with 87 percent attending. Percentages of those completing elementary school are much lower. At the middle and high school level, the enrollment figure dropped to 44 percent, while for higher education, the enrollment rate was only 4 percent.

More than half the population is literate (54 percent in 2006), but this varies between males and females and from region to region. Progress is being made: in elementary, middle, and high schools, the government introduced a modern curriculum, which includes math, information technology, sciences, Urdu, and English, and Pakistan now has 130 universities in contrast to two in 1947.

## Education and religion

Madrassas are private schools that teach an Islamic curriculum. Critics argue that they encourage extremism and violence, but supporters say that they are just like theological seminaries in other countries. The madrassas account for between 1 and 3 percent of all schools in Pakistan. The government has set up an education board to regulate and register the madrassas, but it remains uncertain how successful this will be.

These students at a madrassa in Karachi are taking their mid-year exams. About 6,000 young men and women are fed, housed, and taught at this religious school.

## Health and welfare

Basic welfare and health care provision in Pakistan varies from region to region. Some sanitation improvements have been made recently, and there is greater access to water, but rural areas still lag behind the cities. Where there is poor sanitation, the risk of waterborne illness increases: diarrhea remains a serious health problem, as are diseases such as tuberculosis and polio. In 2007, UNICEF calculated the infant mortality rate for children under age one in Pakistan as 73 per 1,000. This is a very high rate since similar statistics for Western European

**These women, in a slum area of Lahore, are carrying cans of water on their heads. Lack of clean water presents a big health risk throughout the country.**

countries are usually around or below five per 1,000. According to United Nations figures, life expectancy in Pakistan is 64.5 years, and so Pakistan ranks 136 out of 195 countries.

Most people in Pakistan use private health care, and only 23 percent of the population rely on the public health service. There are just under a thousand public hospitals in the whole country and 73,000 private health providers.

## FOCUS: WOMEN IN GOVERNMENT

Pakistan's constitution encourages women's participation in all aspects of work and leisure, and gender discrimination is now prohibited by law. A proportion of seats in the National Assembly is reserved exclusively for women candidates, and in the 2008 general election, 60 women were elected to serve as members of the National Assembly. Women regularly achieve high office in Pakistan's political system: Benazir Bhutto, the former prime minister, is perhaps the most famous, but there are many others, such as Famida Mirza, of the Pakistan People's Party, who was elected the first female speaker of the National Assembly in 2008.

## The role of women

The role of women in modern Pakistan is varied. While in some areas their role is very traditional and centers around household duties and child rearing, the overall picture is more complex. In urban areas, many women have professional careers in medicine, law, and business. More than 60 members of the National Assembly are women, representing a range of political parties, including the Pakistan Muslim League. In some of the provinces, the practice of purdah, where women are largely confined to the home, is predominant. In these areas, women often wear the chador or burka, which covers them from head to foot. In rural areas such as the Punjab and Sindh, women work in the fields. There is little or no segregation of the sexes, but women wear a dupatta, a scarf that covers the head and shoulders.

Pakistan has been criticized for failing to protect women's human rights, but it has set about changing its laws. Honor killings have attracted much attention from human rights activists. An honor killing is the murder of an individual by other family members when it is believed that they have brought shame on the family (usually because of disapproved sexual or romantic relationships). Recently, the government made the practice of honor killings illegal. Change is gradual, and the reality is that there are differing views in Pakistani society about what a woman's place in society should be.

**These Pakistani women carry torches during a rally in Lahore to celebrate World Labor Day. The rally was held to demand the government improve the conditions and wages of working women in Pakistan.**

## Popular culture

Pakistan has a growing urban middle class and is increasingly open to Western cultural influences. This is leading to change in the type of popular culture and leisure interests that appeal to young Pakistanis.

## Music and film

There are many traditional forms of folk music in Pakistan that are influenced by Persian, Arabic and Turkish music and that use traditional instruments such as the sitar and sarod. However, traditional styles are changing, and new types of music are becoming popular in the towns and cities. A new generation of Pakistani musicians has blended traditional music with modern Western styles to make distinctive pop and rock music. Pakistani musicians have produced their own versions of hip-hop and rap, and there is a genre called Sufi rock, made famous by the band Junoon.

Pakistan also has its own film industry, based mainly around Lahore and popularly referred to as "Lollywood" in contrast to India's "Bollywood." There are film production centers in Karachi and Peshawar (Kariwood and Pollywood) and an annual film festival in Karachi. Television and radio are increasing in popularity as a relaxation of media law allows more television and radio stations to grow. There are now several private TV stations showing Western, Asian, and domestically produced programs.

**Film actress Sana Nawaz dances on the set of a Lollywood film. Sana is one of the most successful screen heroines in Pakistan. In the background, a musician plays the sitar.**

## Sport

The most popular sports in Pakistan are hockey, cricket, polo, and squash. Hockey is the national sport, and Pakistan has won gold medals at three Olympic Games and gold at the Hockey World Cup four times.

Cricket is the most popular game, and it is controlled by the Pakistan Cricket Board (PCB). The importance of cricket in Pakistan is underscored by the fact that the president of Pakistan acts as the patron of the PCB and appoints the PCB chairman, the top official of the game in Pakistan. There is great cricketing rivalry with India, and at times politicians have tried to use cricket to improve relations between the two countries, giving rise to the phrase "cricket diplomacy." But Pakistan continues to be a mix of old and new, and many other sports are played, from soccer, to auto racing, to the traditional team sport of *kabaddi*, a type of tag wrestling.

**Here Pakistani and Indian wrestlers compete in a bout of *kabbadi*. This team sport originated on the Indian subcontinent. Team members on a playing field make "raids" into the opposing team's territory, while holding their breath, to "tag" their opponents.**

### FOCUS: CRICKET AND POLITICS

Like other sports, cricket can arouse strong passions. On occasion, spectators have resorted to protest and violence, attacking players and even digging up the field. Politicians have been quick to use cricket as a diplomatic tool. In 1960, cricket tours between Pakistan and India were suspended for 18 years, and since then, Pakistan has twice refused to let its team tour India. President Zia used cricket as a way to meet Indian politicians informally in the 1980s, and in 2005, President Musharraf met Indian politicians at a cricket match to discuss Kashmir. More alarmingly, in 2009, six policemen and two civilians were killed when terrorists attacked the Sri Lankan cricket team playing at Lahore.

# CHAPTER 4

# Political Changes

Pakistan's progress toward democracy since independence has not been without problems. The main reasons for this are the nature of the constitution, the importance of religion in Pakistan, and the number of political factions in the country.

## Political foundations

Pakistan's first constitution was written in 1956. Officially, it announced the country would be an Islamic republic with a president, prime minister, an executive with a cabinet, and the National Assembly. Since 1956, though, the constitution has been through many changes, particularly regarding the division of power between the president and the prime minister. Although there is a now the Senate as well as the National Assembly, tensions still exist. There are also conflicts between the different regions and the central government. There are still considerable disagreements over the role Islam should play in political life. Some people believe religion should be more of a personal matter; others see it as one of the most important elements in the identity of the Pakistani state. According to the current constitution, the president must be a Muslim.

Here, men offer prayers during Ramadan, the period of fasting, at the King Faisal Mosque in Islamabad. For many in Pakistan, Islam is one of the keystones of the Pakistani state.

These Shia Muslims are carrying a replica of the Imam Ali religious shrine through the streets of Lahore. Imam Ali was the cousin and son-in-law of the prophet Muhammad and is important to all Muslims.

## Religion and politics

The inspiration behind the founding of Pakistan was the creation of a Muslim state where Muslims could live free from discrimination and sectarian violence. The reality has been more complex. Muslims in Pakistan follow two different branches of Islam. The largest group is the Sunni Muslims, who account for about 80 percent of the population. The smaller group of Shia (also known as Shiite) Muslims makes up 20 percent. The Sunni and the Shia have important religious differences, which have led to conflict and violence, making Pakistan hard to govern.

Sectarian groups such as al-Qaeda are Sunni Muslims. They claim that the Shiites are influenced by foreign politicians critical of Islam. The conflict between Sunni and Shia Muslims often leads to violence, and it has been estimated that as many as 4,000 people have died as a result of sectarian violence in the last two decades.

## Politicians and parties

In the 2008 general election for the National Assembly, 340 seats were shared between 10 parties. Political support is divided by religious beliefs, regional affiliations, and other political views. This makes it hard to reach agreement, and parties often form short-lived coalitions, making for a volatile and unpredictable political environment.

After the 2008 election, the two largest parties, the PPP and the PML(N), worked together, but the alliance ended later in 2008 over disagreements about the reinstatement of judges fired by Musharraf.

### Percentage of seats won in the 2008 general election

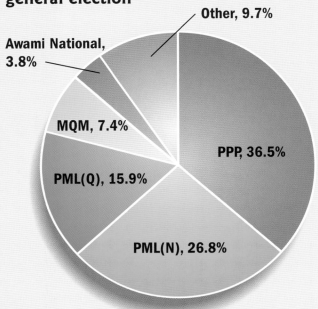

- Other, 9.7%
- Awami National, 3.8%
- MQM, 7.4%
- PPP, 36.5%
- PML(Q), 15.9%
- PML(N), 26.8%

Sources: BBC and Guardian Newspapers Ltd.

## The armed forces

The armed forces of Pakistan, and the army in particular, is one of the largest and strongest institutions in Pakistani society. Defense is of vital importance to the new nation, and the military is a powerful influence in current affairs.

## The military and politics

Since the founding of the nation in 1947, elected leaders have been ousted by military coups three times. For much of its brief history, Pakistan has been ruled by military leaders. Traditionally, senior army officers were drawn from elite social groups. They were prepared to use military force to safeguard what they saw as Pakistan's national interests and security. In the past, many senior army officers have felt that politicians are corrupt and that the Pakistani system of government,

### FOCUS: THE ISI—PAKISTAN INTELLIGENCE AGENCY

The Directorate for Inter-Services Intelligence (ISI) was formed in 1948. Its role is to collect information that will help protect the security of Pakistan. During the Soviet invasion of Afghanistan in the 1980s, the ISI, helped by the US Central Intelligence Agency (CIA), supported the Afghan resistance to the Soviets by providing weapons and training. Since then, the ISI's role has been controversial, and the Indian government has claimed it has secretly been supporting Islamic terrorists.

with its fragmented political parties, has made democracy unworkable.

**Women are an important contingent in the Pakistani army. These Rangers stand to attention during a ceremony at the Rangers' headquarters in Karachi.**

## Islam and the military

The extent to which the army has been influenced by Islamic extremism is not easy to assess. Generally, the army has been moderate from a religious standpoint. Some Western analysts think that the number of soldiers who are sympathetic to Islamic militants has increased in recent years. It is possible that the recruitment of more urban, lower-middle-class men to the officer corps has made the army more conservative and more hostile to the West. The generation of officers who served under General Zia ul-Haq, who took the presidency in a coup in 1977 and promoted a policy of the Islamization of Pakistan, were devout, but not militant, Muslims. Today, there are doubts about army loyalty because of an apparent lack of determination in tackling the Taliban in the tribal areas and the NWFP regions.

Ownership of the northern territory of Kashmir is disputed between Pakistan and India and is the source of much conflict between the two countries. In 1999, India launched massive air strikes from Kargil against Muslim guerrillas from Pakistan.

## Criticism and withdrawal

The army has been the focus of criticism both from within Pakistan and from other countries. In Pakistan, the army's reputation suffered after defeats against India in 1947 and 1971, and its withdrawal from Kargil, in Kashmir, in 1999 was another loss of face. The army has also faced domestic and international criticism for its attempts to exert control over Islamic extremists.

Domestically, some Pakistanis see it as repressing Muslims. Internationally, the army is seen as being sympathetic to extremists. In 2008, though, the new chief of staff, General Kayani, took a fresh approach, ordering officers to keep out of politics.

## From autocracy to democracy

In 1999, General Pervez Musharraf seized power in a military coup and appointed himself chief executive. Later, he assumed the title of president, promising that military rule would be temporary.

## Musharraf in power

Musharraf's period of office saw the continuation of factional conflicts. The leader of the Pakistan Muslim League (PML), Nawaz Sharif, was convicted of corruption but later pardoned and deported. Soon after the September 2001 attack on the World Trade Center, Musharraf announced that Pakistan would support the US-led "War on Terror." As a result, Musharraf became increasingly unpopular and appeared unable to unite and stabilize the country. While political and sectarian violence continued under Musharraf's rule, he remained both president and head of the army, angering opponents who considered him too powerful.

## Conflict and the law

In 2007, Pakistan's supreme court reviewed whether or not Musharraf could legally be president and head of the army. The chief justice, Iftikhar Chaudhry, who was in charge of the review, was suspended on charges of nepotism, but this attempt to control the judiciary by Musharraf backfired and support for him declined.

During his time in office, Pervez Musharraf had to balance US demands to curb extremism and growing anti-American feeling among Muslims in Pakistan.

Benazir Bhutto was the first woman elected to rule a Muslim country. She was the daughter of ex-president and prime minister Zulfikar Ali Bhutto. Benazir held the post of prime minister twice, from 1988–1990 and again from 1993–1996.

return to Pakistan to campaign. However, the campaign was marred when Benazir Bhutto, leader of the Pakistan People's Party (PPP), was assassinated. The PPP and the PML won a majority of seats and formed a coalition government, forcing Musharraf to resign. Benazir Bhutto's widower, Asif Ali Zardari, was later elected president. Chief Justice Chaudhry and other judges were reinstated in 2009, and the new government swiftly agreed to a truce with Islamist militants in the tribal areas and NWFP.

Opposition to Musharraf grew, and as a result, he agreed to hold an election for the presidency and stand down as army chief of staff. Later in 2007, an election was held, which Musharraf won, though some argue it was because the opposition boycotted the elections. The Supreme Court of Pakistan was on the verge of ruling the election result illegal when Musharraf fired the judges, appointed a new Supreme Court, and declared a state of emergency.

## Return to democracy

Recognizing that the situation had to be resolved, Musharraf announced that fresh elections would be held. PML leader Nawaz Sharif was allowed to

### FOCUS: THE NWFP

The North-West Frontier Province is the smallest of Pakistan's four provinces and is about the same size as Maine. The region is home to the Pashtuns, and kinship is organized on the basis of membership of tribal groups. The NWFP is seen as an area of strong support for the Taliban, and there is a strong sense of independence in the region. This has made it difficult to govern, and in recent years, the Pakistan army has intervened in the region, fighting against militant Islamists.

# CHAPTER 5

# Economic Changes

Pakistan's economy is one of the top 50 in the world and was the third-fastest-growing economy in Asia in 2005. It is a low-income economy, but Pakistan has been earmarked as having the potential to become one of the world's largest economies in the twenty-first century.

## Changes in the economy

Traditionally, Pakistan's economy has been based on agriculture. In 1947, agriculture accounted for 53 percent of Pakistan's wealth as measured by gross domestic product (GDP). In recent years, agriculture has shrunk to 20 percent of GDP, while the service and manufacturing sectors have grown. Pakistan has an enormous cotton textile industry and is the world's third-biggest exporter of cotton. Pakistan also exports clothing, carpets, rice, leather, and chemicals. Major imports include gas, machinery, and transportation equipment. Pakistan's fledgling car industry, while accounting for 3 percent of GDP in 2007, is set to grow significantly in the future.

## Economic resources

Pakistan isn't rich in natural resources, but it does have the advantage of plentiful supplies of natural gas. Compressed natural gas technology

**These women are harvesing wheat on the outskirts of Hyderabad. About 25 percent of Pakistan's land is under cultivation, and wheat is the main crop.**

Old and new mix on Chundrigar Road in the heart of Karachi's financial district. In addition to the financial institutions, Chundrigar Road is home to Pakistan's biggest circulating newspapers, TV channels, the stock exchange, and Rangers headquarters.

(CNG) is a growth area for Pakistan, which has a network of nearly 3,000 stations nationwide, employing 30,000 people. The CNG industry has helped cushion Pakistan from the effects of increased oil prices that have affected other countries.

**The structure of Pakistan's economy, 2007**

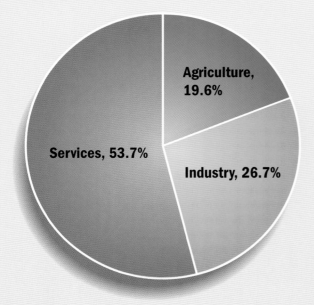

Agriculture, 19.6%

Services, 53.7%

Industry, 26.7%

Source: World Bank

Pakistan has a growing population and a labor force of 49 million people. Population growth can be a disadvantage, putting pressure on scarce resources. The average life expectancy in Pakistan is a modest 64.5 years, and the adult literacy rate is only 49 percent. But an expanding young population gives Pakistan the advantage of low labor costs in comparison to its competitors.

## Government policy

Successive governments in Pakistan have been eager to maintain and develop economic growth. A key element in plans for growth is to follow the Chinese policy of producing goods cheaply and then exporting them to foreign markets. This enables Pakistan to take advantage of one of its greatest resources: cheap labor. The government has also tried to encourage high-tech industry by giving favorable tax breaks to companies and removing duties and by increasing spending on development and improving the country's infrastructure.

**Successful economic policies have led to sustained growth in Pakistan. In 2005, the World Bank identified Pakistan as one of the top 10 reformed economies in the world.**

## Transportation and communications

Pakistan has made tremendous progress in developing its transportation and communications infrastructure in recent years. Because it is a large country, fast and efficient transportation and communication links are vital for successful economic development.

## Rail and road

Pakistan's rail network was first developed by the British and was built primarily for the benefit of the military. This has hampered the usefulness of Pakistan's rail network ever since, even though much has changed since that time. Trains carry about 65 million passengers per year, and there are some 200 freight stations on a 5,061-mile (8,163-km) network. There is only one metropolitan rail system similar to those in Western countries, the Karachi Circular Railway, but that has not been completed, and plans for a subway in Lahore have not been realized.

A great deal of effort has been made to develop the road infrastructure. Pakistan built the first superhighway in south Asia, the M2, which opened in 1997 and links Islamabad and Lahore. More superhighways have been added since then, and there are also 22 highways, which carry about 75 percent of all commercial traffic in Pakistan.

**The Karakoram Highway is the highest paved road in the world at 15,393 feet (4,693 m) and links Pakistan with China. Trucks and tractor-drawn carts are still widely used in rural areas to transport goods, and often they are ornately decorated and painted.**

## Air and sea

Pakistan has a total of 139 airports, 95 of which have paved runways. The most important airports are those in the larger cities: Karachi, Lahore, Islamabad, Peshawar, and Quetta. The most important internal air routes are those linking Lahore, Islamabad, and Karachi. There are several Pakistani airlines and many international flights making air travel easy between Pakistan and the rest of the world.

The largest port in Pakistan is Port Karachi, followed closely by its neighbor, Port Qasim. Together, they handle 95 percent of cargo entering or leaving Pakistan, and both are equipped to take very large freight vessels and container ships. A third major port has been developed at Gwadar in Balochistan. This port is intended to provide a

**This container ship is docked in Port Karachi. The port is postioned on the north shores of the Arabian Sea, close to major shipping routes such as the Strait of Hormuz.**

deepwater terminal for the region and an easy route for trade from the Arabian Sea through to China. The aim is to build oil and gas terminals at the port.

## Communications

Communications infrastructure is growing rapidly in Pakistan, particularly in urban areas. Broadband Internet access is available in the cities, and Pakistan has one of the highest rates of cell phone use in south Asia: about 90 million out of a population of 170 million own a cell phone.

## An industrial revolution

In recent years, Pakistan's economy has modernized. Karachi, Lahore, and other cities have expanded, and investment has been made in modern industries such as car manufacturing, information technlogy, oil and gas exploration, and service sector industries.

## Manufacturing industry

Pakistan's car industry has grown tremendously in recent years. The Pakistan Automotive Manufacturers Association (PAMA) has 20 member companies and in 2007 employed a

**Technicians work on the first Pakistani car, the Revo, at a plant near Karachi. Made by the Adam Motor Company, the four-door car will cost about 15,000 Pakistani rupees—less than the cheapest Japanese-made alternative.**

workforce of just over 7,500. Many of the member companies are joint partnerships with large foreign manufacturers such as Chevrolet, Suzuki, and Honda. These companies are a vital part of an industry that employs 192,000 people across all sectors, manufacturing and supplying parts to PAMA members. The automobile industry generates 16 percent of the wealth of the manufacturing sector as a whole, and that pace is expected to continue.

## The service sector

The service sector of the economy, which does not produce goods but provides essential services to businesses and consumers, has also expanded. In 2007, it produced 53 percent of Pakistan's GDP. Service sector businesses that have been particularly successful in Pakistan have been

**This boy is shaping mud bricks at a brick factory in north Pakistan. The government has recently passed laws limiting child labour, but these laws are almost always disregarded.**

particularly in rural areas, which reduces the average amount earned across the country to $1,027 per year. Around 24 percent of the population lives below the poverty line, although this is a decrease of 10 percent from levels in 2000–1.

## Future prospects

Pakistan has the potential for economic growth. For this to happen, it will be important for the country to develop its manufacturing sector and to start exporting more than it imports. It will also be necessary to reduce its foreign debt and stabilize Pakistan's currency, the Pakistani rupee.

transportation, finance, banking and insurance, information technology, services, and communications provision and storage.

## Economic growth and inequality

Growth in the service sector has helped the creation of a prosperous urban middle class in Pakistan. Some experts estimate that about 30 million people fall into this category and earn incomes averaging around $10,000 per year. However, there is a high level of poverty,

### FOCUS: CHILD LABOR

Despite changes in the law, child labor remains a problem in Pakistan. The International Labor Organization estimates that 3 million children are used as cheap labor working in the textile industry or making sports equipment. The United Nations (UN) and the Pakistani government have tried to eliminate the practice, but in poor areas, many people continue to see child labor as a solution to poverty.

# CHAPTER 6

# Environmental Changes

Rapid population growth in the cities and increasing poverty means that pressures on the environment are intensified in Pakistan. In cities, population growth has led to urban congestion, a fall in the quality of the air and water, and waste management problems. In rural areas, there are problems of deforestation, crop failure, desertification, and a decline in biodiversity.

## Air quality

Rapid expansion of the population and a huge increase in traffic in cities has led to a deterioration in air quality in Pakistan. The large number of motorcycles and diesel-powered trucks, which use poor quality fuel, creates higher levels of pollution. According to the World Health Organisation (WHO), air pollution in Karachi and Lahore is 20 times higher than WHO standards, and the Pakistan Economic Survey of 2007 stated that the levels of dust and smoke particles in the air are five times higher than levels in the developed world. In rural areas, indoor pollution is created by burning wood and biomass material.

## Water pollution

With an agrarian economy and rapidly growing cities, Pakistan faces increasing pressure on its water supply. In 2007, the Pakistan Economic Survey calculated that 54 percent of the population had access to safe sanitation and

**The Indus River is the main source of drinking water in Pakistan, though it is badly polluted in parts and contaminated by heavy metals. The Indus is also used to irrigate the Punjab, the center of Pakistan's agricultural industry.**

## COMPARING COUNTRIES—$CO_2$ EMISSIONS, 2004 (MILLION TONS)

| | |
|---|---|
| US | 6,587 |
| Japan | 1,415 |
| Germany | 975 |
| UK | 618 |
| France | 459 |
| Pakistan | 139 |

Source: United Nations Statistics Division

66 percent had access to safe drinking water. However, as demand for water has increased, so has water pollution. Anti-pollution laws are poorly enforced, and factories often dump toxic effluent into main water supplies. In 2006, thousands of people reported feeling ill after drinking polluted water, and numerous deaths were reported. In some cities, local authorities have been unable to afford the cost of adding chlorine to the water supply.

## Government policies

The Pakistan government has taken several steps to tackle the environmental problems facing the country. One policy has been to encourage the use of compressed natural gas in place of gasoline and diesel. There are now approximately 1 million CNG vehicles in Pakistan, making it the third-highest user in the world, behind Argentina and Brazil. Pakistan has had its National Environmental Action Plan since 2001 and has also committed to international environmental agreements, pledging itself to the UN Millennium Development Goals. In order to meet the problem of water shortages, the government has proposed building approximately 6,000 water purification plants around the country.

NATURAL GAS

CNG

**CNG is seen as a way to continue modernizing the economy while minimizing environmental damage. CNG is made from natural gases, such as methane, and although it produces greenhouse gases, it emits much less $CO_2$ than other fuels.**

## Earthquakes

Pakistan has a rugged environment and is particularly susceptible to a range of natural environmental hazards.

Within or near its borders, Pakistan has the largest mountain ranges in the world. These mountains were created at the meeting point of the Eurasian and Indian tectonic plates. The Indian plate has been sliding underneath the Eurasian plate for many centuries, and the resulting pressures frequently result in earthquakes in the region.

In recent years, there have been several earthquakes in Balochistan (1935, 1945, 2008), in Hunza (1974), and in Kashmir and the Hindu

**These men are praying in front of a mosque in Balakot, northern Pakistan, that was destroyed in the 2005 earthquake. Tens of thousands of people were left homeless in the mountains just before winter.**

Kush (2005). Most of these earthquakes have been graded as strong to major. The Kashmir earthquake of 2005 is estimated to have killed 74,000 people in Pakistan, while the figure for the 2008 quake in Balochistan was about 300.

Natural disasters such as earthquakes can have important social and political implications. The response to the 2005 earthquake was both slow and inadequate, leading to criticism of President Musharraf and his government.

## Floods and droughts

With a growing population, water supply is a crucial issue for Pakistan, yet the extreme variations in climate make regulating the water supply difficult. More than two-thirds of Pakistan's agriculture—much of it in the fertile Punjab and Sindh plains—is dependent on irrigation, but Pakistan's climate makes both flooding and drought common.

In 2007, flooding during the monsoon season killed 200 in Balochistan and another 200 in Karachi. Thousands of people were left without fresh water supplies or electricity for days. Then, in 2008, monsoon rain in the northern Punjab forced thousands of people from their homes. Large-scale schemes such as the Tarbela and Mangla dams have done much to improve the water supply, but it is not easy to tame the elements in Pakistan.

### FOCUS: THE INDUS RIVER

At 1,686 miles (2,720 km) long, the Indus is the longest river in Pakistan, flowing from its source in the Himalyas near Tibet to the Arabian Sea near Karachi. About 80 percent of Pakistan's agricultural production is in the Indus River basin, so water supply from the Indus River system is vital. At partition from India in 1947, the upper basin of the Indus lay on India's side of the border, and in 1948, India cut the flow of water to the irrigation canals on the Pakistan side. The Indus Waters Treaty of 1960 gives India exclusive use of all the waters of the eastern rivers and Pakistan use of all the western rivers.

**This is the Tarbela Dam, which sits on the Indus River. It rises 485 feet (148 m) high and is 8,997 feet (2,743 m) in length. Projects such as this help to regulate Pakistan's water supply and ensure that the country is less susceptible to drought.**

# CHAPTER 7

# Changing Relationships

Pakistan's relationships with the major world powers are shaped by its strategic location, its importance as a Muslim nation, and its relationship with India.

## Pakistan and the major world powers

Pakistan's relations with Russia have been tense since the Russians generally support India in disputes with Pakistan. Pakistan borders Tajikistan, which was once part of the Soviet Union, and therefore it is not in Russia's interests to have a strong Pakistan. When the Soviet Union invaded Afghanistan in 1979, Pakistan actively supported the Afghan resistance. Pakistan has usually been allied with the US, the Soviet Union's great rival from the end of World War II to the end of the Cold War in 1991. In the twenty-first century, relations with China have become important as China becomes a major world power. Pakistan has a border with China, and the countries have good diplomatic relations. The two countries have a defense pact, and China sells arms to Pakistan.

## Pakistan and India

India and Pakistan have had a difficult relationship since 1947. Part of the reason for the formation of Pakistan was to create a separate Muslim state, which would allow Muslims to maintain their identity and culture.

**Every evening at the Pakistan-India border near Lahore, an elaborate show of bravado is staged by the border guards. Here, the Pakistani guards are in black and the Indians are in brown. Crowds gather at the border to watch the spectacle and cheer.**

**President Musharraf (third from the right) poses with officials in 2004 before the launch of a nuclear-capable missile with a range of up to 930 miles (1,500 km). India and other countries have voiced their concerns about Pakistan's nuclear capabilities.**

India is a predominantly Hindu country. Cultural differences and territorial arguments between these two large neighboring countries have led to frequent conflicts. A major source of tension has been territorial claims to Kashmir in the north. This dispute has resulted in war on three occasions: first in 1948, then in 1965, and again in 1999. Currently, the area is partitioned, and both countries have large numbers of troops stationed there.

In 1971, India fought against Pakistan in the East and West Pakistan conflict and was influential in creating the new state of Bangladesh from what had been East Pakistan. Since the 1970s, relations between the two countries have varied. Islamist terrorist activity has made both countries suspicious of each other, with each country accusing the other of supporting terrorist attacks.

## COMPARING COUNTRIES: PAKISTAN AND INDIA, KEY MILITARY DATA

|  | Pakistan | India |
|---|---|---|
| Armed forces personnel | 619,000 | 1,288,000 |
| Combat aircraft | 376 | 599 |
| Tanks | 2,461 | 4,059 |
| Submarines | 8 | 16 |
| Ships | 6 | 48 |
| Nuclear warheads | 30–60 | 50–90 |
| Military spending as % of GDP | 3.1 | 2.3 |

Sources: BBC, IISS 2008, *Jane's Country Risk* and *SIPRI Yearbook* 2006

## Pakistan—a nuclear power

Pakistan and India started developing nuclear weapons in the 1970s and successfully tested devices in the late 1990s. There is international concern about the danger of a nuclear confrontation between the two countries, and Pakistan has also been accused of helping other countries develop nuclear weapons.

## The War on Terror

The War on Terror refers to the response of the US and its allies to the terrorist attack on the World Trade Center on September 11, 2001. Al-Qaeda, which is headquartered in Afghanistan and is also protected by the Taliban, claimed responsibility for the attack. In response, the US took a range of military action; including sending troops to Afghanistan in 2001 and to Iraq in 2003.

## Pakistan's role

Since Pakistan shares a border with Afghanistan, it has been the focus of activity in the War on Terror. The North Atlantic Treaty Organization (NATO) and US forces have claimed that Taliban guerrillas fighting in Afghanistan frequently cross the border into Pakistan, where they find support and refuge. The US and its allies have sought help from the Pakistan government to curb Islamist militants. Not everyone in the NWFP and FATA is an Islamist militant, but many people are sympathetic to the Taliban and al-Qaeda for upholding the Muslim faith. Al-Qaeda is known to have run training camps in the NWFP. The Pakistani government has attempted to remove

On September 11, 2001, two passenger airplanes were hijacked and flown into the Twin Towers of the World Trade Center in New York. Two other planes were also hijacked and subsequently crashed. Al-Qaeda claimed responsibility for the attacks.

Islamist militants from the area, sending in police and large numbers of troops to the NWFP and

## FOCUS: WHO ARE THE TALIBAN AND AL-QAEDA?

The Taliban is a Sunni Islamist movement that ruled Afghanistan for five years before US, British, and armed forces from other countries drove them out under the leadership of NATO in 2001. The US, UK, and NATO are now fighting a guerrilla war in Afghanistan while the Pakistani government has responsibility for the northwestern region of Pakistan. Al-Qaeda is another Sunni Islamist movement, led by Osama bin Laden. It is dedicated to freeing Muslim countries from Western influence and is known to run training camps in the northern border areas of Pakistan. Al-Qaeda claimed responsibility for the September 11 bombing.

FATA. However, these are not areas where the Pakistan armed forces can always count on local support.

## International criticism

US and allied forces have attacked Taliban outposts in Pakistan, leading to complaints from Pakistan. The US and other Western governments have been critical of Pakistan's attempts to impose control in the NWFP. Some critics suggest that Pakistan is in danger of becoming a failed state. Others claim that elements within the Pakistani government (particularly the ISI) secretly support the Taliban, though there is no evidence to support this view. Despite receiving large sums of money for military aid from the US, the Pakistani government has had limited success fighting a guerrilla war against a highly motivated enemy.

**The Swat Valley in the NWFP is a Taliban stronghold and is the scene for battles between the army and insurgents. As many as 200,000 civilians have fled the war zone.**

# CHAPTER 8

# Future Challenges

**P**akistan is a country with great potential, but it now faces a crucial period in its history. Once again, Pakistan finds itself at the center of relations between east and west.

## Islamic fundamentalism

The rise of Islamic fundamentalism is probably the greatest challenge facing Pakistan. It is of great international importance, and how Pakistan deals with this issue has an impact far beyond its own borders. Pakistan's leaders face the difficult task of diffusing the deep tensions between Islamic fundamentalists and more moderate Muslim opinion and other social groups. Meanwhile, terrorist activity has become a serious threat.

In the north, the Taliban are accused of burning down girls' schools and assassinating teachers. The Taliban want to see Pakistan ruled according to strict Islamic principles and sharia law. Islamic fundamentalists believe that women should play a traditional role in society and that modern education for girls has no place in an Islamic society.

The Pakistan government has found it difficult to govern the region, but in 2009, the Zardari government permitted the use of sharia law in the NWFP as a concession to Islamist opinion. However, the Taliban are not universally popular in the north, and reports in the second half of 2009 indicated that local support was fading because of violence. The conflict is probably not one that can be resolved quickly.

**There is a strong movement by religious moderates in Pakistan against the Talibanization of the north. These Sunni Muslims in Lahore are protesting against religious extremism.**

## Toward democracy

In addition to facing the challenges posed by radical Islamists, Pakistan is having to develop its own democracy rapidly. This has been difficult when there are so many political parties: politicians have to do deals, and there is a good deal of fighting between factions. Political infighting has led to frequent charges of corruption against prominent politicians. The constitution has also been unhelpful at times, concentrating too much power in the hands of the president. All these factors make for an uncertain political future and make it difficult for the government to act with authority.

## A fresh start

The current president, Asif Zardari, was elected in September 2008 after Pervez Musharraf conceded to pressure to step down and hold elections. Zardari promised to work with his political rival

**The US held talks with Pakistan and Afghanistan in 2009 in an attempt to resolve the international dispute. Here, Secretary of State Hillary Clinton is pictured with President Asif Ali Zardari.**

Nawaz Sharif and to reinstate 60 judges dismissed by Musharraf. However, Zardari was slow to reinstate the chief justice, fueling suspicion that he was worried the chief justice would bring corruption charges against him. President Zardari faces a big challenge. He has to construct a democratic political system that will have the confidence of the whole population. He also has to tackle militant Islamists, deal with a separatist movement in Balochistan, and try to develop the economy. Pakistan's future is only partly in its own hands. Other countries; social, religious, and political movements; and political leaders will play a vital part in defining Pakistan's future role in the world.

# Timeline

**2600–1800 BCE** Indus Valley Civilization.

**514 BCE** Persians invade.

**326 BCE** Alexander the Great conquers the Indus Valley.

**c. 711 CE** Arabs invade and bring Islam to the country.

**1525** Beginning of the Mughal dynasty.

**1615** East India Company establishes trading posts on the subcontinent.

**1757** Beginning of British rule on the subcontinent.

**1940** Muslim League demands a separate state for Muslims.

**1947** British Parliament agrees to partition of the Indian subcontinent and independence for India. East and West Pakistan also created.

**1958** Military coup—General Mohammed Ayub Khan assumes presidency.

**1965** War with India over Kashmir.

**1969** General Agha Mohammed Yahya Khan assumes presidency.

**1971** Civil war (India also involved). East Pakistan becomes Bangladesh.

**1978** General Zia ul-Haq proclaims martial law and assumes presidency.

**1988** President Zia dies in airplane crash.

**1998** Pakistan tests its first nuclear bomb.

**1999** Kargil conflict in Kashmir.

**1999** General Pervez Musharraf stages military coup.

**2007** Benazir Bhutto assassinated.

**2008** President Musharraf resigns, Asif Ali Zardari elected president.

# Glossary

**agrarian economy** An economy based on farming.

**biomass** Plant materials and animal waste used as a source of fuel.

**buffer zone** A strip of land which is left empty and separates two countries in dispute.

**British Commonwealth** An inter-governmental organization consisting of 53 independent member states, most of which were previously parts of the British Empire. The head of the Commonwealth is a ceremonial position held by Queen Elizabeth II.

**compressed natural gas (CNG)** A fossil fuel substitute for gas and diesel that is cleaner than those fuels.

**coup (d'état), or military coup** A sudden and often violent overthrow of a government.

**cricket** A game played with a ball and bat by two sides of players centering on two wickets, each defended by a batsman.

**defense pact** An agreement between two or more countries to defend each other if one is attacked.

**desertification** The process by which land turns into arid desert, usually as a result of human activity, such as overpopulation, overgrazing, or extracting too much water from the ground.

**gross domestic product (GDP)** A way of measuring the amount of wealth a country produces.

**guerrilla war** An unconventional form of warfare where a smaller force uses ambushes and raids to attack a larger and better-armed, conventional force.

**Hindus** People who follow Hinduism, the third largest religion in the world and the largest on the Indian subcontinent.

**Indian subcontinent** Another term used to describe all of south Asia; the southern region of the Asian continent.

**infrastructure** The basic physical and organizational structures needed for a society in order to work, such as roads, water, power, sewage and waste systems, telecommunications systems, rail networks, and airports.

**Islamist** A Muslim who believes that Islam should govern all aspects of life.

**Islamization** The implementation of Islamic law in all areas of social, economic, and politcal life.

**Islamic fundamentalism** A term used to describe those people who believe that society should be governed strictly according to Islamic principles.

**kabbadi** A game that is like a form of tag wrestling played by two teams of seven.

**madrassa**  An Islamic religious school.

**monsoon season**  A seasonal wind that brings heavy rainfall. The southwest monsoon period falls between June and September, and there is another monsoon season during October and November.

**Muhajirs**  Pakistani citizens who came to the country from India. Many are found in elite social positions.

**North Atlantic Treaty Organization (NATO)**  A military alliance of 28 countries from Europe and North America.

**Pashtuns (also known as Pathans)**  Ethnic Afghans, many of whom also live in the north of Pakistan, in areas such as the NWFP.

**polo**  A team sport somewhat like hockey but played on horseback. Originated in Persia and developed by the British in India.

**purdah**  The rules that forbid women to be seen by men.

**sectarian violence**  Violence between groups of people who are divided by a deep hostility to religious or political views that are different from their own.

**separatist movement**  A group that promotes cultural and political separation from a larger group and the formation of a new nation.

**sharia law**  Islamic religious law.

**shawal kameez**  Traditional dress worn by men and women in south Asia. Consists of pants and a long shirt or tunic.

**Shia (or Shiites)**  Describes Muslims who follow the Shia branch of Islam. Shia Muslims believe that religious authority can lie only with direct descendants of the prophet Muhammad.

**Sikhs**  Followers of Sikhism, who follow the teachings of Guru Nanak. The fifth-largest organized religion in the world.

**Sufi rock**  A type of Pakistan rock music that fuses rock with Sufi music and ideas. Sufism is a type of Islamic mysticism—or a search for spiritual truth.

**Sunni**  Describes Muslims who follow the Sunni branch of Islam. Sunni Muslims believe that religious authority lies with the person best able to uphold the customs and traditions of Islam and not necessarily with direct descendants of the prophet Muhammad.

**Taliban**  An Islamic movement that ruled Afghanistan from 1996 to 2001 and is still active in that country and Pakistan.

**UNICEF**  The United Nations Children's Fund.

# Further information

## Books

Bhutto, Benazir. *Daughter of the East: an autobiography.* Simon and Schuster, 2007.

Jones, Owen Bennett . *Pakistan: Eye of the Storm.* Yale University Press, 2002.

Kwek, Karen. *Welcome to Pakistan.* Franklin Watts, 2005.

Musharraf, Pervez. *In the Line of Fire: A Memoir.* Free Press, 2006.

Robinson, Francis. *The Cambridge Encyclopedia of India, Pakistan, Sri Lanka, Nepal, Bhutan and the Maldives.* Cambridge University Press, 1989.

## Websites

http://news.bbc.co.uk/1/hi/world/south_asia/country_profiles/1157960.stm
BBC country profile with information and links

http://www.guardian.co.uk/world/pakistan
Continually updated news page from the *Guardian*, London

http://www.pak.gov.pk/default.aspx
Pakistan government's Ministry of Information website with links and profiles

http://www.radio.gov.pk/
Radio Pakistan

http://thenews.jang.com.pk/
The *International News*—Pakistan newspaper published online and in English

http://pakistaniat.com/
All things Pakistan—a blog that gives the flavor of the reality of modern Pakistan

# Index